"You have seen how man
was made a slave;
You shall see how a slave
was made a man."

Frederick Douglass

FREDERICK'S JOURNEY

The Life of Frederick Douglass

BY DOREEN RAPPAPORT

ILLUSTRATED BY LONDON LADD

 Disney • JUMP AT THE SUN

LOS ANGELES   NEW YORK

Frederick was taken from his mother
when he was a baby and
sent to live with his grandparents.
His mother slaved six days a week
from sunrise to sunset
on another farm twelve miles away.
She longed to see Frederick, but
walking the twenty four miles round trip
and getting back by dawn
was almost impossible.
Only five times did he feel
her loving arms around him.

*"I do not recollect ever seeing my mother
by light of day. She would lie down with me
and get me to sleep but long before I waked,
she was gone."*

He heard whispers that a man
named Old Master was his father.
But he was never sure.

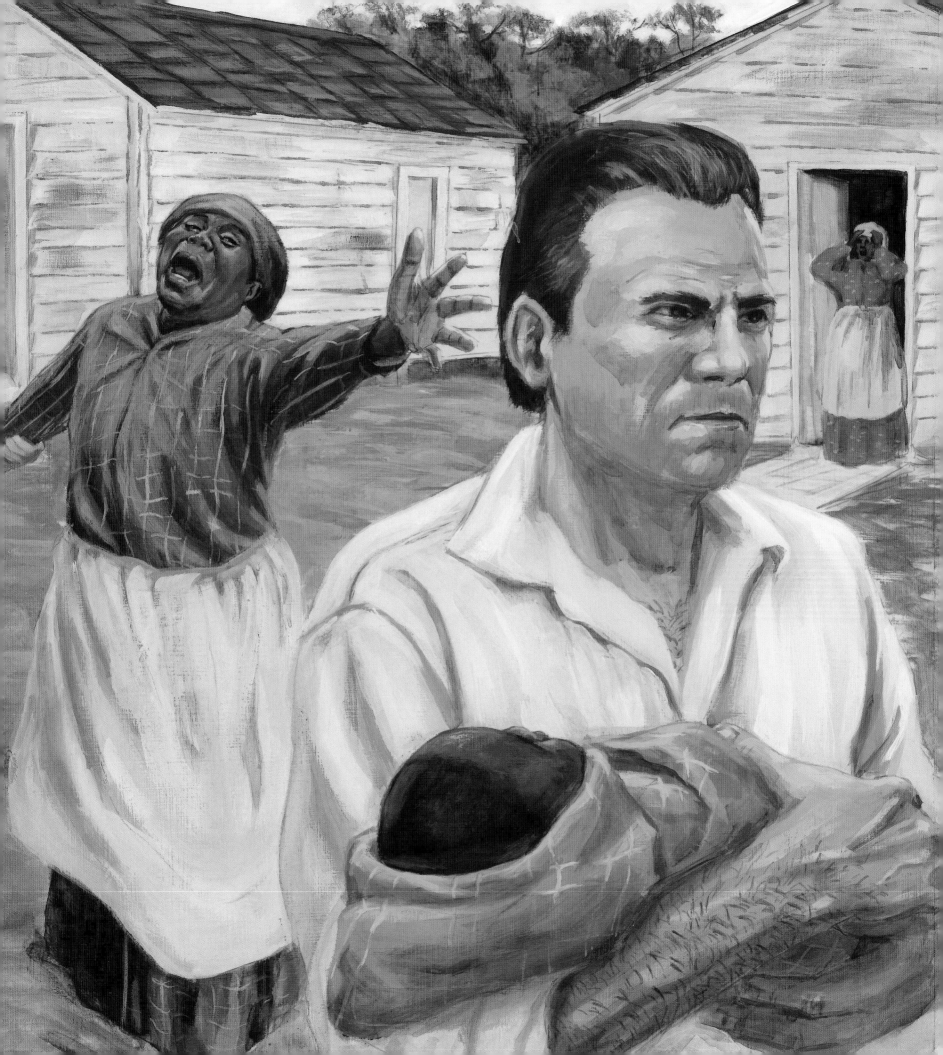

Grandfather Isaac was free.
Grandmother Betsey was a slave.
She cared for all her grandchildren,
knowing how painful it would be
when she had to give them up.

Her loving hands bathed Frederick,
fed him, nursed him, and hugged him.
He ran freely among the cornstalks,
which tickled his face and legs.
He watched squirrels scamper up trees
and bury their nuts in the earth.
Grandmamma taught him to fish.
He dipped his thread line and pin hook
into the water but got only nibbles,
while she scooped up scores of
shad with her handmade nets.

"Living with my grandmother,
whose kindness and love
stood in place of my mother's,
it was some time before
I knew myself to be a slave."

The summer he was six,
his owner ordered his grandmother
to bring Frederick to him.
Her loving hand trembled as they walked
twelve miles to a place with grand houses
and hundreds of black men, women, and children.

"They are kin to you,"
Grandmamma said, pointing to three children.
"Go and play with them."

*"I really did not understand
what they were to me, or I to them.
Brothers and sisters we were by blood.
But slavery had made us strangers."*

Frederick feared that if he played with them,
his grandmother would leave without him.
She did, and he wept.

"Grandmamma was all the world to me."

Old Master made Frederick
sleep on a clay floor in a closet,
covered by a coarse blanket.
His only clothing was an itchy shirt.
He ate sitting on his naked behind,
and with an oyster-shell spoon
scooped up cornmeal mush
out of a trough.

"*The children were called to eat, like so many pigs.*
He that ate fastest got most.
I have often been so pinched with hunger,
that I fought with the dog
for the smallest crumbs."

Frederick's mother died when he was seven.
He was never even told she was ill.

One morning, screaming woke him.
Old Master was shouting ugly words
and whipping Frederick's Aunt Esther.

*"I was hushed, terrified, stunned,
and could do nothing.
Her fate might be mine next."*

He saw more beatings and
a few times felt the whip on his back.
Another aunt ran away.
Try as Old Master did,
he could not find her.

*"Her success made me
seriously think of escape."*

After two years, Old Master gifted Frederick
to relatives in Baltimore, Maryland.
Free blacks lived and worked there.
His new mistress, Sophia Auld, gave him
a clean shirt and pants to wear.
He ate at a table now and
slept in a straw bed with a cover.
He cared for Mistress Sophia's two-year-old, Tommy.
In his free time, he was allowed
to play in the neighborhood
with poor white boys his age.

Mistress Sophia taught him
the alphabet and simple words
so he could read the Bible.
Her husband was furious,
insisting that reading
*"will forever unfit him
for the duties of a slave."*
She stopped teaching him.

But Frederick sensed that words had power.
While the family slept,
he sneaked into the library and
sounded out words in books.
With his white playmates,
he traded food for words
in his copy book.

*"For a single biscuit,
my hungry little comrades
would give me a lesson
more valuable than bread."*

Day by day, month by month,
year by year, harder and harder words.
He could not stop, even though
he risked whippings if found out.

Frederick read newspapers he found in the street.
He copied letters with chalk
on fences and sidewalks and barrels.
He polished boots for money and
bought a book of speeches about freedom.
How wondrous to learn that people
used words to teach and convince,
and that some white people hated slavery!

"There was HOPE in those words."

Six years later, Fredrick was returned to his old master,
who died the following year.
Frederick's new master found him
"too uppity" for a slave.
He had to be taught a lesson.
He rented Frederick to a farmer
who starved him, worked him, and whipped him
until his spirit was broken and
he stopped dreaming of freedom.
Then one day Frederick fought back.
He knew he might be killed for doing so.

*"This battle was the turning-point
in my life as a slave. I was a MAN now.
It inspired me with a renewed
determination to be A FREE MAN."*

The farmer never touched him again.

His new master sent Frederick back to Baltimore,
where he fell in love with Anna Murray.
But it was hopeless to think of marriage.
He was a slave; Anna was a free black.
For them to be together,
Frederick would have to escape to the North.
Anna would follow.

His first attempt failed.
The second time, he posed as a free seaman.
He jumped onto a moving train heading north.
The conductor asked for his papers and
didn't realize that his papers described someone else.

Train, steamboat, train.
Finally he arrived in New York City.

"Free earth under my feet!
A new world."

Frederick sent for Anna, and they married.

They moved to New Bedford, Massachusetts.

He took a new last name, Douglass,

to make it more difficult for his owner

to track him down.

Soon he was lecturing in states

as far west as Indiana and Illinois.

He spoke about his life as a slave

and about prejudice in the North.

"I went in pursuit of a job of caulking

but such was the prejudice against color,

that white caulkers refused to work with me."

Many Northern whites did not like what he said.

They threw eggs at him and beat him up.

But nothing stopped him from speaking the truth.

Many white people did not believe
that Frederick, who spoke so well,
could have ever been a slave.

He wanted people to believe him,
so he wrote his autobiography.
He did not shy away from
naming his owner and describing
the places where he'd lived.
His friends warned that this put him in danger.
He did it anyway. His book became a best seller.

Now his owner knew where he was.
Frederick unhappily left his family and
went to Great Britain and Ireland,
where slavery was outlawed.
For the first time in his life,
he felt truly free.

*"I have spent some of the happiest
moments of my life in this country."*

Two years later, friends bought Frederick
his freedom for $710.96.
He returned home and started a newspaper
named *The North Star*, because slaves
followed that star to freedom.

In articles and speeches,
he insisted that *all* Americans
should have equal rights.
His words angered some people.

"I hold that women, as well as men,
have the right to vote."

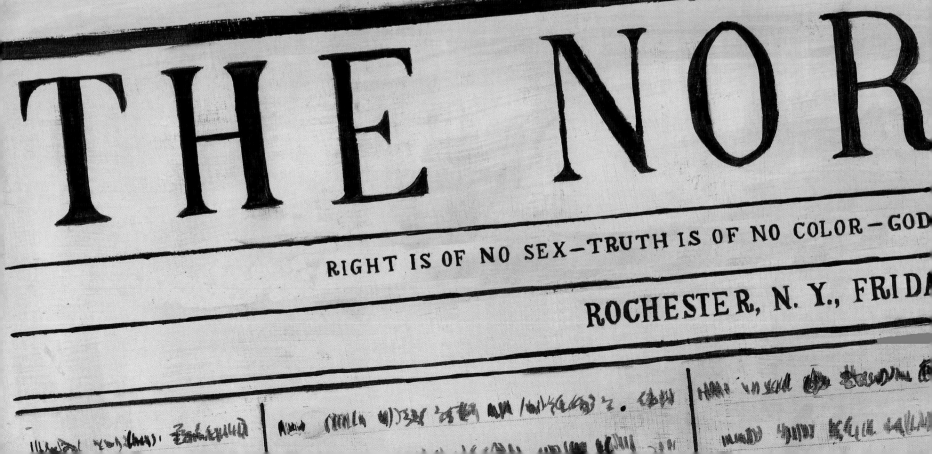

THE NOR

RIGHT IS OF NO SEX—TRUTH IS OF NO COLOR—GOD

ROCHESTER, N. Y., FRIDA

"What, to the American slave,
is your Fourth of July?
This 4th of July is yours, not mine.
You may rejoice, I must mourn."

TH STAR.

IS THE FATHER OF US ALL, AND ALL WE ARE BRETHREN.

DECEMBER 3 1847.

It was a crime to help runaway slaves.
Frederick admired Harriet Tubman,
a former slave, who risked her life,
to lead others to freedom.
He wrote her:

*"The midnight sky and the silent
stars have been the witness
of your devotion to freedom."*

Anna and Frederick defied the law, too.
They became conductors on
the Underground Railroad and
hid whoever knocked on their door.

The issue of slavery exploded into
civil war between the North and South.
President Lincoln had said many times
that slavery was evil, but insisted
he did not have the power to end it.
After two years of war, he changed
his mind and issued the
Emancipation Proclamation.
It freed millions of black Americans.

Frederick cheered with thousands
when the news was announced.

"I never saw Joy before.
Men, women, young and old, were up;
hats and bonnets were in the air."

Frederick insisted that black men
be allowed to fight for their freedom.
He traveled from town to town,
urging them to join the Union Army.
Thousands signed up, including
his sons Lewis and Charles.

Black soldiers got only half pay
and were given inferior weapons.
The South often killed captured black soldiers.
Douglass met with Lincoln and
insisted that they be protected.

"*He did not let me feel for a moment
that there was any difference
in the color of our skins!
I am satisfied now that he is doing all
that circumstances permit him to do.*"

After four years, the North won the war.
But Frederick's happiness was marred
when Lincoln was killed.

Slavery was now ended everywhere
in the United States.
But Frederick saw more work ahead.

*"Slavery is not abolished
until the black man has the ballot."*

The new president, Andrew Johnson,
did not agree with Frederick.
So Frederick took to the road again
to convince others.
It took four more years until
the lawmakers agreed to give black men the vote.

Douglass had traveled far—
from slave to free man,
from illiterate to educated,
from powerless to powerful.
It had been a difficult journey.

He knew his people faced
more difficulties ahead.
He often reminded them:

*"What is possible for me
is possible for you."*

Author's Note

I first learned about Frederick Douglass in 1965 when I went to McComb, Mississippi, to teach in a Freedom School. That summer, along with meeting contemporary black heroes who were risking their lives to vote and encourage others to vote, I began to learn about African American heroes of the past. Frederick Douglass astounded me with his determination and brilliance.

Researching this book gave me the chance to meet Douglass again. I reread the detailed records that he left about his life and struggles. It thrilled me to rediscover his imaginative and resolute path to learning to read, and his growing understanding that words have power—to do good as well as evil. As it had fifty years ago, it pained me to read about his despair over his hideous treatment by Edward Covey, which temporarily destroyed even his dreaming of freedom, for I know that experience was shared by so many enslaved Africans.

As a writer, I believe in the power of words to teach and persuade. Douglass used words to educate white Americans about the evils of slavery and to encourage other black Americans to believe that all human beings have the strength within them to be reborn, even under the most dire of circumstances. I am honored to have had the chance to write his biography.

—Doreen Rappaport

Illustrator's Note

I thought I knew a lot about Frederick Douglass, but as I started working on this book, I was surprised at the depth of his lifelong commitment to standing against racism and injustice, not only toward African Americans but toward anyone experiencing discrimination. I admired that Frederick was a man who was determined to let no obstacle stand in his way. He wasn't afraid to disagree and speak his mind, even to the president of the United States. I would like to think that if he were alive today, he would be in the forefront, speaking up against any type of injustice.

To really try to understand Frederick Douglass, I dove deep for my research. I read his autobiography and took detailed notes, and I would sometimes listen to an audio version while sketching and painting. I spent countless hours poring over hundreds of documents in nineteenth-century archives, traveling to places he lived, like Baltimore, Boston, and his home in Washington, D.C., and visiting his grave in Mount Hope Cemetery in Rochester, New York. To really get into character, I grew my hair long like his and learned how to tie a necktie nineteenth-century style so I could pose for my own photo reference. I would stand in the mirror and recite certain lines from his speeches and practice his intense stare. It became a passionate labor of love to illustrate Frederick's life.

—London Ladd

Important Dates

1818

Frederick Augustus Washington Bailey is born on Holme Hill Farm, Tuckahoe, in Talbot County, Maryland, to Harriet Bailey. There are rumors that his owner is his father.

1819–1824

He lives with his grandparents, Isaac and Betsey Bailey.

1825

His mother dies when he is seven or eight. He lives with Old Master, Captain Aaron Anthony.

1826

He is sent to live with Hugh and Sophia Auld in Baltimore.

1826

Old Master dies. Frederick's new master is Thomas Auld.

1834

Thomas Auld sends Frederick to Edward Covey, known for "breaking" difficult slaves.

1836

He is sent again to live with Hugh and Sophia Auld.

September 1838

He escapes to New York, marries Anna Murray, and changes his name to Frederick Douglass. Frederick and Anna have five children: Rosetta, b. June 24, 1839; Lewis Henry, b. Oct. 9, 1840; Frederick Jr., b. March 3, 1842; Charles Remond, b. Oct. 21, 1844; Annie, b. March 22, 1849.

August 1841–45

Douglass goes on lecture tours for the American Anti-Slavery Society.

May 1845

His first autobiography, *The Narrative of the Life of Frederick Douglass*, is published.

May 1845–47

He tours Great Britain and Ireland.

December 1847

He starts *The North Star*.

1850

Frederick and Anna become involved in the Underground Railroad.

April 12, 1861

The Civil War begins.

January 1, 1863

Lincoln signs the Emancipation Proclamation, freeing all slaves in rebellious states and territories.

1863

He meets with President Abraham Lincoln to discuss the treatment of black soldiers during the Civil War.

June 2, 1865

The Civil War ends.

March 1870

The Fifteenth Amendment is adopted, giving black men the right to vote.

1874

Douglass becomes president of the Freedman's Savings and Trust Company.

1881

He is appointed recorder of deeds for Washington, D.C.

August 1882

Anna Murray Douglass dies.

January 1884

Douglass marries Helen Pitts.

February 20, 1895

Douglass dies at age seventy-seven in Washington, D.C.

Selected Research Sources

Blight, David W. *Frederick Douglass and Abraham Lincoln: A Relationship in Language, Politics and Memory.* Milwaukee: Marquette University, 2001.

—— *Frederick Douglass' Civil War: Keeping Faith in Jubilee.* Baton Rouge: Louisiana State University Press, 1989.

Douglass, Frederick. *Narrative of the Life of Frederick Douglass: An American Slave.* Cambridge: Belknap Press of Harvard University, 1960.

—— *My Bondage and My Freedom.* New York: Random House, 2003.

Eaton, John, in collaboration with Ethel Osgood Mason. *Grant, Lincoln and the Freedmen: Reminiscences of the Civil War.* New York: Longmans, Green and Co., 1907.

Foner, Philip S. *The Life and Writings of Frederick Douglass: Early Years 1817–1849.* New York: International Publishers, 1950.

Huggins, Nathan Irvin. *Slave and Citizen: The Life of Frederick Douglass.* Boston: Little, Brown, 1980.

Oakes, James. *The Radical and the Republican: Frederick Douglass, Abraham Lincoln and the Triumph of Anti-Slavery Politics.* New York: W. W. Norton, 2007.

Preston, Dickson. *Young Frederick Douglass: The Maryland Years.* Baltimore: Johns Hopkins University Press, 1985.

Quarles, Benjamin. *Frederick Douglass.* Washington, D.C.: The Associated Publishers, Inc., 1948.

If you want to learn more about Frederick Douglass, read:

Cline-Ransome, Lesa. *Words Set Me Free: The Story of Young Frederick Douglass.* Illustrated by James E. Ransome. New York: Simon & Schuster/Paula Wiseman Books, 2012.

Collier, James Lincoln. *The Frederick Douglass You Never Knew.* Illustrated by Greg Copeland. New York: Children's Press, 2003.

Lutz, Norma Jean. *Frederick Douglass.* Philadelphia: Chelsea House, 2001.

McKissack, Patricia and Frederick. *Frederick Douglass: Leader Against Slavery.* Berkeley Heights, New Jersey: Enslow Publishers, 2002.

Websites

Narrative of the Life of Frederick Douglass:
www.gutenberg.org/files/23/23-h/23-h.htm

Frederick Douglass National Historic Site:
www.cr.nps.gov/museum/exhibits/douglass

The History Place, Great Speeches Collection:
www.historyplace.com/speeches/douglass.htm

Frederick Douglass on PBS:
www.pbs.org./wbgh/aia/part4/4p1539.html

Frederick Douglass Papers Edition:
www.iupui.edu/~douglass/

For Faith Hamlin, with thanks

—D.R.

To my wife, Theresa.
Thank you for all your love and support.

—L.L.

Text copyright © 2015 by Doreen Rappaport
Illustrations copyright © 2015 by London Ladd
Book design by Maria Elias

First Edition, November 2015

10 9 8 7 6 5 4 3 2 1

H106-9333-5-15258

Printed in Malaysia

Library of Congress Cataloging-in-Publication Data

Rappaport, Doreen.
Frederick's journey : the life of Frederick Douglass / by Doreen Rappaport ; illustrated by London Ladd.—First edition.
pages cm.—(Big words)

ISBN 978-1-4231-1438-3—ISBN 1-4231-1438-8

1. Douglass, Frederick, 1818–1895—Juvenile literature. 2. Abolitionists—United States—Biography—Juvenile literature. 3. African American abolitionists—Biography—Juvenile literature. 4. Antislavery movements—United States—Juvenile literature. I. Ladd, London, illustrator. II. Title.

E449.D75R37 2016
973.8092—dc23
[B]   2014034335

Reinforced binding

Visit www.DisneyBooks.com

In many instances, quotes by Frederick Douglass have been shortened without changing their meaning. Punctuation has been simplified. The quotes on the front endpapers, pages 6, 8, 13, and 26 come from *The Narrative of the Life of Frederick Douglass, An American Slave*. The quotes on pages 11, 15, 17, 19, 20, 22, 25, and 29 are from *My Bondage and My Freedom*. The quote ("I hold that women . . .") on page 30 is from a speech, "What the Black Man Wants," given before the Massachusetts Anti-Slavery Society in Boston, April 1865. The quote on page 31 is from a speech in Rochester, New York, July 4, 1852. The quote on page 32 is from a letter Douglass wrote to Harriet Tubman, Rochester, New York, August 29, 1868. The quote on page 35 is from an 1863 Cooper Institute speech in New York City. The quote on page 37 is from John Eaton's *Grant, Lincoln and the Freedmen: Reminiscences of the Civil War*. The quote on page 39 is from a speech to the American Anti-Slavery Society, 1865. The quote on page 41 is from a talk given to African American students at a school in Maryland, and the back endpaper quote is from a speech given on August 3, 1875, at Canandaigua, New York.

"If there is no struggle, there is no progress."